First Published 2015
©2015 Pentti M. Rautaharju
Original Finnish Poetry by Eino Leino

Seventy Seven Sentiments

A Selection of Eino Leino's Poems

Translated by Pentti M. Rautaharju

TABLE OF CONTENTS

Dedication   vi
Achnowledgments   vii
About Eino Leino   ix
About this collection of translated Leino's poems   xi
About the translator   xiii

SONGS OF MAY (MAALISKUUN LAULUJA, 1896)
The Groan of the Forsaken (Hyljätyn Valitus)   1
In Love (Rakastunut)   2
In Worries Sighing (Huolissaan Huokaileva)   3

THE NIGHTJAR (YÕKEHRÄÄJÄ, 1897)   5
Stockingmind (Sukkamieli)   5
Autumn Sentiment (Syystunnelma)   7
What Is that Song on the Waves? (Mikä On Laulu Lainehilla)   8
Mussel Shells (Näkinkengät Ne Rannalla Narskui)   9
Freezing Feeling (Miks Tuli Mun Äkkiä Kylmä Nyt)   10
The Oil Is Running Out (Jo Loppuvi Õljy Mun Lampustain)   11
Under the Rowan (Pihlajan Alla)   12
The Nightjar (Yõkehrääjä)   14
Asleep in the Forest (Metsään Nukkunut)   15
Flimsy Heart (Hatara Sydän)   17
She Walks as if Over Flowers (Hän Kulkevi Kuin Yli Kukkien)   18

MULTI-COLORED CANE (KIRJOKEPPI, 1897)   19
Molded by Water (Veen Valamia)   19
The Hymn of Vimpele (Vimpelin Virsi)   20
I Push my Boat on the Waves (Mä Lykkään Purteni Laineillen)   21

ONE HUNDRED AND ONE SONGS (SATA JA YKSI LAULUA, 1898)   23
On Alderleaves My Songs I Embroyder (Lepän Lehdille Lauluja Kirjailen)   23

The Sea in the Moonshine (Meri Kuutamolla)   24
When I Reminisce (Kun Muistelen)   26
Seita (Seita)   28
Apple Blossoms (Omenankukat)   29
Morning Song (Aamulaulu)   30
A Small Ballad (Pieni Ballaadi)   31
The Paleface Moon (Kuu Kalpea)   32
I Wanted to Search the Heaven and Earth (Olen Tahtonut Tutkia Taivaan Ja Maan)   33
I Believed that You Were My Happiness (Minä Luulin Sun Elosi Onneksi)   34
Kiss Me Once and Kiss Me Twice (Mua Suutele Kerran Ja Suutele Kaks)   35
Your Laugh (Sun Naurusi)   36
Who Is She? (Kuka Hän On?)   37
Home Again (Taas Kotona)   38
The Sailor in his Cabin (Merimies Kajutassaan)   39
Peace (Rauha) 40
I Dreamt of the Summer (Näin Unta Kesästä Kerran)   42
I Felt as if We Were Rowing (Minust' Oli Kuin Olisi Soudettu)   44
Was it a String that Snapped?(Se Oliko Kieli Jok' Katkesi?)   46
I Lost My Faith and My Hope (Minä Uskoni, Toivoni Hukkasini)   47

FROM THE WAVES OF TIME (AJAN AALLOILTA, 1899)   49
Burial Song (Hautalaulu)   49
The Night (Yö)   50

HYMNS OF THE SKIER (HIIHTÄJÄN VIRSIÄ, 1900)   51
I Stared the Fire Too Long (Tuijotin Tulehen Kauvan)   51
The Strain of the Years (Ja Vuodet Ne Käy Yhä Vaikeammaks)   53
The Song About Happiness (Laulu Onnesta)   55
I Was Young (Olin Nuori)   56
The Farmhand of the Death (Kuoleman Renkinä)   57
That Way There, This Way Here (Toisin Siellä, Toisin Täällä)   58

HOLY SPRING (PYHÄ KEVÄT, 1901) 61
Downstream Drifts the Boat (Virta Venhettä Vie)   61
The Song About Love (Laulu Rakkaudesta) 64
What Is More Beautiful? (Kumpi On Kaunihimpi?) 65

WINTER NIGHT (TALVIYÖ, 1905)   67
Nocturne (Nocturne) 67
Windy Dwelling (Tuulinen Sija)   69
Slandering Mouths (Pahat Suut)   71
When We Depart (Erotessa) 73
Fault (Syy) 74
The Vine (Köynnös) 75
Summer Morning (Kesäaamu)   77
They Leave, Should I Grieve? (Menevät, Murehtisinko?)   79

THE FROST (HALLA, 1908)   81
Sinikka's Song (Sinikan Laulu)   81
Consolation of the Singer (Laulajan Lohdutus)   82
Decision (Päätös)   83
Elegy (Elegia)   84
Visitor to Lapland (Lapinkävijä)   88

STARRY DOME (TÄHTITARHA, 1912)   89
Two Kinds of Eyes (Kahdet Silmät) 89
The Insulted (Loukatut)   92
Clearest Spring (Kevät Kirkkahing) 94
Summer Evening's Gentle Breeze (Suvi-Illan Vieno Tuuli) 95

THE SUNSET (PAINUVA PÄIVÄ, 1914) 97
The Sunset (Painuva Päivä) 97
Autumn Leaves (Syyslehtiä) 100

THE BEAUTY OF LIFE (ELÄMÄN KOREUS, 1915) 103
The Swell (Maininkeja)   103

CAMPFIRES (LEIRIVALKEAT, 1917) 105
Evening Sentiment (Iltatunnelma) 105

LOVE SONGS (LEMMENLAULUJA, 1919) 107
I Wander the Trails in the Forest (Minä Metsän Polkuja Kuljen) 107
Those Eyes(Ne Silmät) 108

WHEN THE LILACS ARE BLOSSOMING (SYREENIEN KUKKIESSA, 1920) 109
Autumn Morning (Syys-Aamu) 109

SHEMEIKA'S SORROW (SHEMEIKAN MURHE, 1924) 111
The Goodness (Hyvyys) 111
The Child of July (Heinäkuun Lapsi) 113
The Sickle of the Moon (Kuun Sirppi) 114
Delusion (Harha) 115

A REMEMBRANCE (ERÄS MUISTO, OUTSIDE REGULAR COLLECTIONS, 1925) 117
1.The Star (1.Tähti) 117
2. The Ray and the Crystal (2. Säde Ja Kristalli) 118
3. Swan Lake (3. Joutsenjärvi) 119

*The poems are listed in chronological order of the publication year of the source collections, with Finnish titles of the poems in brackets.

Dedicated to my daughter Satu Runa,
the fountain for my inspiration,
and to my wife, Dr Farida Rautaharju,
for her unfailing support and encouragement
throughout my retirement years.

My thanks are due to Mr. Esko Piippo, Chairman of the Eino Leino Society of Kainuu, for permission to use the photos from the Paltaniemi-pamphlet of the society. Other photos were contributed by Asa Lyytinen, Kari Antila and Satu Runa who also designed the cover page.

Eino Leino (1878-1926)

This collection of 77 short poems of Eino Leino represents a narrow selection of the vast spectrum of Leino's literary production during his short, multifaceted and tumultuous public and personal life. Eino Leino is justifiably idolized by the Finnish poetry lovers as the greatest poet of the Finnish written languish, following in the footsteps of the vast oral tradition of Finnish epic poets and rune singers documented in "Kalevala". Leino started writing poems already in his teens, and he was 18 years old when his first major collection was published, followed by 31 other poetic collections among other literary works. Leino was the leading force in the creation of the foundation of the Finnish poetry during its formative years amid the rising nationalism of the nation aspiring for independence during the last period of the Czarist Russia.

Twenty of the 77 poems selected come from the 1898 collection Sata ja Yksi Laulua (One Hundred and One Songs). The poems in that early collection reveal romantic, often melancholic sensations of the young poet, still optimistic and enthusiastic about a better mankind. Leino's poems commonly reflect mystic symbolism, duality of love and betrayal, deep passionate love and desperation of love lost, life and death, beliefs and doubts of the searcher of truth. They also reflect the closeness of the poet to the nature around his childhood home on the northern shore of Oulujärvi, a large lake in North-Central Finland. These sentiments are reflected in the following lines translated from Leino's poem Nocturne: *I'm not merry, I'm not sad, I don't weep, but bring me the forrest's shadows, / the shine of the cloud where the day drowns, / the shimmer of the windy hill still asleep, / twinflower's fragrance, reflections on the lake; / the song of my heart from them I make.*

Leino's life cycled through periods from celebrated acclaim and elation of the spirit to extreme frustration, poverty and rejection. As a fiery activist in the evolving cultural, social and political life of the Finnish society, Leino was a sharp critic of the prevailing establishment at any given period, and the elite turned at times strongly against him. His three marriages all failed almost from the beginning. The poet was unyieldingly clinging to the freedom of his personal life, and at the end the freedom of his spirit was the only thing left from his idealism. A few loyal friends tried to sustain his spirit through the turbulent cycles of his life and the periods of deep depressions. He escaped to extremes of bohemian life that gradually ruined his health. Eino Leino died in 1926 at age of 47 years.

The photos above by Esko Piippo from Eino Leino Society of Kainuu show the Sunset at Lake Oulujärvi (below), and a small bay of the lake, Hövelõnlahti, the surroundings of Eilo Leino's birthplace.

About this collection of translated poems of Eino Leino

Translation of poems is always a demanding task. This is particularly true in attempts to translate Finnish poems into English because of the intricacies of the Finnish language which is rich with descriptive words and expressions that often have no counterpart in English. Finnish words tend to be long. Each noun has 16 cases with different endings in everyday use. The adjectives are inflected same way as the nouns and at the same time the base of various types of verbs changes differently. Differing ending of each of the 16 cases actually facilitates composing poems with a formal classic structure in Finnish. In English translation however, it is more difficult to make the translated poems rhyme and to retain the metric because of the vast structural differences of these two languages. The English product is at best, an adaptation.

Leino's poems have inspired musicians and vocalist, and many of them have been adapted in Finnish as musical compositions, 18 of them by Oskar Merikanto. Notable among the most popular productions has been Eino Leino Album by Vesa-Matti Loiri (1978, produced by Flamingo Corp., musical composition Perttu Hietanen). It is an additional challenge for the translator of these particular poems to retain the metric and rhyming to facilitate the use of the lyrics by potential English-speaking performers.

The poems selected are in chronological order of the publication year of the source collections. The Finnish titles of the poems are listed in the Table of Contents (in brackets).

About the Translator

Dr. Rautaharju was born in Finland in 1932. He was nearly 40 years a professor and a career scientist in heart research in Canada and the U.S. Recipient of several academic and other honorary awards, honorary doctorates and the award of Commander, Order of Lyon's Cross of Finland. After his retirement in 2002 Dr. Rautaharju has continued an active heart research program, and as a diversion, translation of classic Finnish poetry including Eino Leino's poems contained in this collection.

Dr. Pentti Rautaharju in front of the Kunst Museum, Munich, July 6, 2010. *Photo by Satu Runa.*

SONGS OF MAY (1896)

The Groan of the Forsaken

One evening when walking a path on the moor,
I gathered heathers, a bunch of four.

The night was magical, the wind was sleeping,
The heather fragrant, the cuckoo calling.

Then suddenly my heart was filled with tears –
My memories flew back to the youth-time years.

Watching the heathers thick and fair,
Reminded me of my maiden's hair.

To the ditch my beautiful heathers I tossed-
The joy of my life in the soil I once lost.

In Love

Early morning's wave is singing brightly
When it loudly splashing shoreline beats,
Aspen leaves there flutter jubilantly,
Free of stress of mankind's daily needs.
Ladybug her sorrows alone churns,
Longing, her own lovely darling yearns.

So did I, like brightest morning waves,
Then a happy child, I was singing,
Playing games like shoreline's aspen leaves,
Playing, singing, loving, dancing.
Ladybug, I lost my gayety,
From you I got this pious melody.

In Worries Sighing

The forest is ringing with singing,
It's loving and mating season,
Jubilant chaffinch and bunting,
As if they lost their reason.

From one tree the birds shy away,
Abhorring, I don't know why.
Under that tree I sit all day,
My worries I sigh and sigh.

THE NIGHTJAR (1897)

Stockingmind

Two shepherds sat at the burn near a pond,
One of them ruddy, the other one blond.

The ruddy-one played his horn joyfully,
The blond-one just sat there quietly.

Then they heard another shepherd to yell:
"Hi fellows, I have some news to tell!

At dawn there, I saw Stockingmind,
You fellows believe me, what a find!

Charmingly-build was her slender body,
Her gait swinging like a melody.

Her eyes were like bluebells ringing,
In her crown yellow mica was shining.

Charmingly smiling she waived to me,
Waived again, it is hard to believe!

Thus exclaimed that shepherd joyously.
The ruddy-one listened longingly:

"To see her once, wouldn't that be something!"
The blond-one just listened, said nothing.

The blond one cried bitterly.
He had seen that fairy already.

Autumn Sentiment

My friend, you were right
When you left me in the night.
Your bosom so young and warm-
By my side a freezing storm.

Look, on the road a flower is paling,
Its petals turning white in the snow.
My dear flower why are you waiting,
It is time to bend down and go.

Memories flashed through my mind
One stays, others away flow:
On my road was a withering flower,
And I covered it under the snow.

What is that Song on the Waves?

What is that song on the waves,
A melody in its wake?
»A craft is riding the billows,
A honeymoon boat on the lake.

Whose bride, I want to know,
Whose wedding fires that glow?
»Cricket's craft, small boats in tow,
Cricket's chosen in the bow.

And the sweetheart of the cricket?
»Ladybird from the alder forest.
Where leads the sweethearts' journey?
»To the ridge on that high island,
In Terhenniemi highland!

Mussel Shells

Mussel shells on the shore crackled
And the blackhaw tree tinkled.
Who walks on the shore rejoicing like that?
Nobody else walks so wicked –

It's my girl, my sweetheart, that's right,
Mussel shells crunching and swinging.
Like a pearl her foot is so white,
I saw it once, ever since adoring.

Freezing Feeling

Why did I suddenly feel so cold,
As if the night got me in it's hold.

Your hands were loving and worm.
Did you leave me in this icy storm?

Did you wish me like an icicle die?
Why did you leave me, why?

The Oil Is Running Out

The flame in my lamp is losing its glow.
Dark is my window, that darkness I know.

I stare and I stare and my thoughts fly high,
They fly and they fly like the bubbles fly.

And bubbles keep wandering everywhere,
The bubble of my happiness is not there.

In the window's darkness only me I see,
No flame in my lamp, in my mind no glee.

Under the Rowan

You became so quiet all of a sudden,
My maiden, your tears started to flow.
Did the cloudy skies you sadden,
Eat your happiness hollow?
The flowers are blossoming carefree,
And the larks are singing their happiness,
So fragrant now is the rowan-tree,
You alone are crying your sadness.

You, in the bud of your youthful days,
Fresh complexion, strong is your chest,
Life beckons you with a smiling face –
Make your life light-hearted, full of zest!
If worries cast shadows on your day,
Or in your hopes clouds will gather,
The glow of my love will chase them away –

Then back comes the kissing weather.
O, please, my beloved, please do not cry,
My maiden, the loveliest, sweetest thing,
The scent of your love gives me a high
Like the rowan-tree in the spring.
I sniff its scent and music starts ringing.
Rowan flowers we together gather
When virgin grass is again growing,
And for us shiny sky, sunny weather.

In winter, here always bitter,
When other berries are falling,
In the rowan-tree also in winter
The waxwing is still singing.
So graceful is rowan's white blossom,
Its berries still prettier, glowing red,
When the nature is winter's ransom
And other berries are frozen dead.

The Nightjar

Once, sitting alone in the evening,
Something in my heart was humming.

What is that humming and humming?
»The maiden is humming and spinning.

I was deep in my thoughts in the evening
When something at my side was singing.

Who is singing so loud, constantly? –
»The death wants the maiden, instantly.

When I was alone in the evening,
I heard my heart crying and sobbing.

Who is there crying and sobbing, ceaselessly? –
»The maiden is crying for her liberty.

Asleep in the Forest

I'm like a child, lost, asleep in the forest,
At twilight waking with a distress cry,
But gone are the brother, and the sister drowned,
And echo only hears my distress sigh.

Poor child, doesn't know what time it is,
Doesn't know the path home, where to go.
There are trails in the forest, between tall trees,
Which one leads to mother, so hard to know.

The backwoods are wild, so ghastly, so creepy,
All things so silent, gray, threatening,
No wind here, so quiet, the branches sleepy,
And behind the trees the trolls are peeping.

The child is crying, running, falling down

Gets up, falls down, and gets up once again.

The child is tiny, forest vast all around,

Home is too far, the fight is in vain.

I'm like that child, lost, asleep in the forest

At twilight waking with a distress cry,

But gone is the brother, and the sister drowned,

And echo only hears my distress sigh.

Flimsy Heart

What a pity your heart and you,
Poor girl, and pity me,
Your heart's windows have no louvers
And cold draft blows on your lovers.

I too was in your heart, and found it flimsy,
I stayed there an evening or two.
But it was so drafty and it was so windy –
It was like nothing that I knew.

You don't believe – go inside to get the feeling,
But don't stay long to come back alive.
I wonder how on earth can anything living,
Like your heart, in that cold draft survive.

She Walks as if Over Flowers

She walks as if over a flower-bed
On the wings of a melody mellow,
So tenderly swaying her body and head.
To see her I quietly follow.

As long as my spirit will stay strong
And my melodies keep flowing smoothly,
She can walk on the blue shiny waves of my song
On the flowers of fantasy.

Photo by Kari Antilla

MULTICOLORED CANE (1897)

Molded by Water

The clay on the shore was cracking,

Split by the long-lasting dryness.

The mind of the singer was grieving

Under the load of sadness.

The water tossed and the sun scorched,

The clay, beaten by whether, splashed,

Turbid and cloudy clay was turned

Into small scoops, tiny purses.

And the foggy spirit was molded,

Split into tiny small verses,

For the children of the village to rejoice,

For the maidens of the village to enjoy.

The Hymn of Vimpele

The gentle lily in Vimpele village
Closes slowly its tired eyelids.
The lake is still and the forest sleeps,
Pale moon from behind the cloud peeks
Over the dim shadowy alley,
And the brook that flows in the valley.

The spruce sleeps, the fir dozes,
From the sauna smoke rises.
The night is white and shadowless.
On pliable fur tree's branches
Walks the song of life and dying,
Like a moonscape painting.

I Push My Boat on the Waves

I push my boat on the rolling waves
And I sail across the lake,
Through the straights between the islands,
To a small bay leads my wake.

There, at the shore of that placid bay,
There hides a bird-cherry grove,
The home of the chaffinch and ladybird,
The cradle of songs in the cove.

And there, in that fragrant shady grove
My dark-haired maiden I meet,
The ladybird of my joyful spring,
My song and my spring-flower sweet.

ONE HUNDRED AND ONE SONGS (1898)

On Alderleaves My Songs I Embroider

On alder-leaves my songs I embroider
And toss them to drift in the river.
One leaf lands faraway, another near,
They float in the stream here and there.

If one of the leaflets would soar so high
Above the waves and forever fly,
And if one of my hymns would fly and reach
The fairy island and land on its beach,
To the people there it would sing a new rhyme,
On that fairy island, beyond reach of time:
How a kiss can be a kiss of death
Or a kiss may bring lifesaving breath.

The Sea in the Moonshine

*So bizarre is the mind of mine
Like the sea in the moonshine.
I shun the fuzz of the company,
When alone, I feel so lonely.*

*So vast is my mind, its reach is so high,
The galaxies of the sky,
Holding the whole world like a treasure,
Day and the night all together.*

*Ah, my mother dear if you were alive,
On your lap I would cry and revive!
And your forgiving hand would wipe my tears,
And sooth the sorrows of the years.*

*All wickedness here makes the mankind cry,
Why all this persecution, tell me why,
When Lord made the earth so wonderful,
And everything here so beautiful.*

Why such persecution the mankind binds,
When the sky above is high?
Look up there to find friendly minds,
Up there, in the glorious sky.

When I Reminisce

When I reminisce, many a lonesome night
I was sitting there alone, lonely,
Watching the stars on the sky, side by side
So close together, glittering, lovely.
Then my maiden dear,
Ah, my maiden dear,
I must come close to you, closer
And look at you longer and longer.

When I reminisce how often I've been
Alone wandering in the wilderness.
Sitting there under the evergreens,
Sitting there, sitting so joyless.
Then my maiden dear,
Ah my maiden dear,
I must kiss you, quietly crying
Kiss again with my tears flowing.

When I reminisce, those thoughts I had,
Many thoughts evil and bad
That we together would have avoided,
Fighting together, fighting united.
Then my maiden dear,
Ah my maiden dear,
Love me longer, still longer,
You must love me longer, forever.

Seita

I'm like a heathen with my offering,
You are my divine tree.
If I tell you my secrets whispering,
You do not secretly mock me.

Down there I spread a sheet in the grove
When the full moon starts the offer season,
From the chaff and sins I sift my soul,
And start to fast my body of poison.

Three times my forehead to the ground I knelt,
Dropped the pearls to the Devine,
Took off my precious buckle-belt.

I'm praying and hope for a sign.
But in silence stands Seita, the God of the night.
And I'm alone, all alone with my faith and plight.

Apple Blossoms

Like apple blossoms my happiness grew
In the luminous nights of the spring,
When the fir cones have that reddish hue,
At twilight the virgins dream.

Those couple of nights around Whitsuntide,
Those spring nights are so deep and so light.
If only my blossoms from wind could hide,
The fruits would grow until ripe.

Ah, heavenly forces please let it be calm
I pray, but your plans may not agree!
My almighty savior, hear my psalm:
Save orphan's own apple tree!

Morning Song

Echo my song, echo and soar
Echo and soar higher.
In twilight the waves billow
Under the shoreline' willow.

Sleep my youthful heart and dream,
Young is still the night.
See all nature's creations
Awakening at twilight.

Fly my love and soar sky high
Fly high over the mountain.
Mountains, nothing can defy
Two love birds from loving.

A Small Ballad

Under the window a pine tree swayed,
The girl looked out of the window.
»Where on earth in the ways of the wind
Is my dearest wandering now?

The winds were beating the old pine tree,
Mighty sorrows the fiancé.
»I wonder whose funeral music now
The organs of the wind are wailing.

Heavy winds razed and broke the pine tree,
The bride was cut by the yearning.
The fiancé in foreign lands,
Faltering and withering.

The Paleface Moon

The paleface moon on its eternal flight,
The spring-night is lovely and sacred.
Together here we still sit in the night –
Though long ago we should have parted.

The breeze in the night sings its serenades
To the twigs of the sleepy alder.
The heart beats, silently anticipates
Those glorious dreams of the summer.

I Wanted to Search the Heaven and Earth

I wanted the heaven and earth to search
To find the fountain of truth.
Now I want only your eyes to search,
Two heavenly stars of the youth.

Hush, hear this, this is wholly true,
Down like a dove my love soars,
And now when I sit here next to you,
And kiss your lips, my heart roars!

I Believed that You Were My Happiness

I believed that you were my life's happiness
But you were my whole life and its flavor,
Guiding us through joyful togetherness,
Yet also through pain and sorrow.

I believed that you would my spirit lift,
But you were the fairy of sleep.
You brought roses from the valley as a gift,
- And icy snow from the mountain peak.

I thought you were the lightning in my nights,
But you were the night itself.
A velvety black gown hides your delights
But you brighten the skies with your eyes.

Kiss Me Once and Kiss Me Twice

Kiss me once and kiss me more,
More kisses and more loving,
I believe in the dream we had before
Of a carefree tomorrow coming.

When you lean your head on my chest
You hear roaring surge of the rapids.
When the waves of love sway your hips
The ecstasy soaks my lips.

Your Laugh

Your laugh is my love and it is my pleasure,
Like the thrush sings its evening song
When dawn sun shows its golden treasure
And the cuckoos are calling along.

Your laugh brings me enchanting harmony,
It rings like the twang of the harp.
Whoever once heard its melody,
It sings in his chest like a lark.

Your laugh brings me fear, it brings me fright
Like the lamb is scared of the butcher.
Whoever heard that laugh falls into night,
And stays in the trance forever.
Your laugh can be tender and atrocious,
And so evil, still so lovingly ring,
Your laugh can be ecstatic, murderous –
Ah, if once more for me it would sing!

Who is she?

Who is she? The moonshine's whisper,
A fairy of the fields, a dream of the forest,
A melody rising from the singer's chest,
Or a night-time dream of the singer?

I don't know, but if a dream she was,
It was a dream from paradise.
If a song from the singer's chest it was,
That song will to heavens rise.

Home Again

I walk like a plowman around his strips
On the ruins of my beloved home,
I reminisce days of my youth, the memories,
Plays joyful and fishing trips.

I walk like a plowman walks on his field,
The heart is full, peace in the chest.
The winter is gone, it had to yield
To summer days mild and blessed.

I want to start from the start again,
I want a new life to begin,
I don't want the fight to strike me down,
I want to stand fighting and win!

I walk like a plowman walks on his field
On the moors and cattle roads beloved.
Sowing new hopes new harvest may yield,
And I water the fields with tears from my heart.

The Sailor in his Cabin

I looked at the lily of the valley,
At its lovely leafs and flowers so white.
Her dark eyes I remembered suddenly,
And her hair, like tropical night.

What is she thinking and where did she go?
Sorrow or joy in her mind and voice?
Do tears of longing from her eyes flow,
Or do they gleam and rejoice?

I do not wish her to be sad and crying,
I do not wish her laughing either.
If like me faraway waves she were looking
It would make my mind a bit brighter.

Peace

What are these fragrant smells around me?
What is this silence, this stillness?
What is the meaning of the peace in my heart,
So new and so strange in its greatness?

I can now hear when the flowers grow,
What the trees to each other whisper.
With hope the dreams mature and flow,
With hope the crops will get crisper.

So quiet around me is everything,
All nature is tender and sweet.
In my heart spring flowers are opening,
Their fragrance is peaceful and deep.

Please let your hem to cover
My heavy, tormented head,
On your lap to rest, and forever
The sorrows of the mind to forget.

The earth is so desolate, empty,
You alone fill the night with a feast,
With twinkling stars you fill the night sky,
In their shine the arteries beat.

I Dreamt of the Summer

Once when I was dreaming,
I dreamed that Lord's sun was shining,
Shined to me, shined to the others,
To the backyards of my poor brothers,
Made green thousands of lentils,
Made blue hundreds of lakes,
Rejoiced the lovely heather-moor
The oak in the woods told its lore,
The tree spoke and the flower knew –
The poor man believed it was true.

He thought his summer had arrived,
He bared his chest open, wide
For soothing touch of the summer,
To hear the hummingbirds hummer.
An angry wind suddenly squealed,
Lonely wolf in the backwoods howled,
Winter sky hurled snow in deep heaps,
People in village spoke icy words.

Never, even once, thereafter

Have I since dreamt of the summer.

I Felt as if We Were Rowing

It felt as if we were rowing
On a shiny lake's surface floating.
The waves had wormed up in the sunshine
And the chest of the cliff at the shoreline.

It felt as if we were drifting and landed
Under that lovely shoreline rock,
And on fine white sand we waded,
And walked to a nearby hillock.

From there we saw a lovely sunset
On straights between tiny islands,
And the evening and night had arrived
Over singing trees in the lowlands?

We saw the haze dancing through the night,
Drifting from the lake to the shore,
Meadow's drowsy ponds swimming behind
And the dream grew bigger and bigger.

The dream was swinging from branch to branch,

And from flower to flower it danced—

We stood there on the hill, hand in hand,

Watching how it tiptoed.

Photo by Satu Runa

Was it a String that Snapped?

Was it a string that so suddenly snapped,
with a strange twang through the air zapped?
Why is that tender blush on your cheeks,
why is that smile on your straberry lips?

My maiden, hiding your face you turn around.
Was it the string of your heart, that sound?
No, it was just a tiny spring flower
that opened up at early morning hour.

I Lost My Faith and My Hope

I lost my hope and my faith died
And I wrecked my ship on the reef.
Your kisses I trust, your eyes will me guide,
And me and my ship in right heading keep.

My girl, if you are still in love with me,
Your kisses will make my sails to ring,
My boat will sail again fully rigged,
And I holler to the wind and sing:

A great many ships are sailing the waves,
A great many stars twinkle in the night.
Cheers, my ship sails with the brightest star,
The lucky star of my bride.

FROM THE WAVES OF TIME (1899)

Burial Song

The stream is restless, the waves rolling restless,
The ocean enchanting, the ocean endless.
    Sleep stream in the lap of the ocean.

The wind is restless and the leaves fly high,
Happy is the leaf that to the valley will fly.
    Sleep leaf in the lap of the valley.

The sunrise arrives and quenches the star.
Not forever quenched is the life that leaves far.
    Sleep star in the lap of the daylight.

The Night

The night comes, the sun dies.
The shroud of the dusk dims the eyes.
In the swamps of the wilderness
The will o' the wisp kindles.

All alone I sit in my dwelling,
My friends shy away from me,
But in the odd estranged dreaming
Is my spirit's jubilee.

Who is there? Who moves in the thicket?
Is that a shroud that sways?
The image rolls and glitters, so wicked,
I know so well all of its features.
My thoughts are frozen still, startled,
The shroud of dusk covers my eyes.

HYMNS OF THE SKIER (1900)

I Stared the Fire Too Long

Way too long I stared at the fire,
The burning logs needed poking.
I was burning with desire,
Dreaming of my dark-haired darling.

Glowing coals an image painted,
Brought back memories elated,
Summer birds soaring in the sky,
Summer days swinging high,
Cheeks were glowing, mouth was smiling –
The eyes for another longing.

I roved lands, I roved wilderness,
Swaps and wilderness endless.
Wilderness hides a bluish smoke,
Under smoke a dwelling remote,

A maiden at her loom sitting,

A golden fabric weaving,

Clattering pearls in the fabric.

For whom is the golden fabric?

»The gift for the bride of the forest.

And the marten-chested bride?

»For the backwoods skier's wedding night.

Not too long should forsaken souls

Stare at the fire, poke flaming coals,

Tears fill the eyes, soul forsaken sobs

Head between the hands fighting tears,

Throat's rattle in ears,

The chest heaves, the heart throbs.

The Strain of the Years

The strain of the years, ever increasing pain,
Sad dreams grow sadder with nostalgic strain,
They burn, they glow and they hold me tight.
Every evening I dream that tomorrow new
Will sooth me, my turmoil subdue!
At dawn old sorrows return after endless night.

They come again as if this was their home,
They bring also their friends in my home to roam,
Their names bring just remembrance faintest.
Yesterday's sorrows, so painfully lashing
Feel sweet now with today's sorrows smashing –
That biggest, when comes the biggest?

You almighty ruler, when will you come near,
You, my highest pain and biggest fear.
Since my childhood for you I have been waiting,
Sleepless at nights, trembling in my bed.
I saw in your eyes an accusing thread

If I ever was happiness searching.

In front of you, facing you I want to kneel,
Look you in the eyes, tell you how I feel:
Take back my life that you gave,
But my young spirit I'll not give, never!
In its pain it strikes its fire, forever,
I will take it with me to my grave!

The Song about Happiness

Who happy is, his happiness should hide,
Who treasure has, should find a hiding-place,
To no-one else his happiness confide,
Its joys and richness all alone embrace.

The gaze of others ruins the happiness,
Who happy is should go to wilderness
To live in quiet loneliness,
 Enjoying quietly his happiness.

I Was Young

I was young and in happiness believed,
In sweet dark eyes and their promises.
My sanity, myself deluded
In hazy dreams and misty reveries.

I relearned the springtime songs to create,
Relearned old notes to recall.
I had a dream of the summer and waited –
Waking up, it was already fall.

I don't accuse your eyes
For losing my sanity!
You cried singing blues
With sympathy, with pity,
When my spirit's last bits and chips
Were killed by your smiling red lips.

The Farmhand of the Death

Along the fields of the Death I was walking,
The Death was plowing and I was crying.

The Death called: "Come-on man, I need a farm-hand!
You get boards for your casket, a piece of land."

I will be your farm-hand, I replied,
The Afterlife, for certain, looks after its child.

From then on the fields of the Death I have plowed –
The years have passed, life's moments escaped.

My friend is far and my heart a frozen clot –
Ah Lord, when do I reach the end of my plot

That Way There, This Way Here

I would like to discuss sometime
With those children of the sunshine,
Joyous children of prime village,
Children of southern vintage,
Those whose spirit has the glow,
From their mouth words smoothly flow,
Their pens like sparkles fly,
Like birds singing in the sky.

To those children I would say:
It's easy sweet music to play
In the midst of a vineyard,
In the shine of the daylight star,
Among the flowers of the spring,
Something else is poems to sing,
Sacred holy fires to light
While trying drifting snow to fight
In this land of frost and night.

If you managed to win an inch
The frost took back without a flinch.

HOLY SPRING (1901)

Downstream Drifts the Boat

Downstream drifts the boat.
Where's the end of the road?
The surge beats the bow and keel.
What is the human –
Restless like will-o' the wisp?
Sandy soil already tries to crab the heel.
One is born to joy, another's life is sad,
And in everybody's heart the timer is counting,
When ticking stops, begins the time for dying.
Downstream drifts the boat.

Where's the end of the road?
The gloom of the sins threatens doom.
For a moment glows man in fame
Then dies down its flame,
A tiny pile of ash is all that remains.

And the sins grow and join other sins,
The son in cradle inherits the sins of the father.
The chest fills up with trash, ash and clutter.
Where's the end of the road?

Downstream drifts the boat,
The whole world as the load.
Ah, eternal sea!
Bring still-water to me.
And you also need a rest, world endless,
Your white-haired head is tired, restless.
Take a note of shaking shadows of death.

Where's the end of the road?
No-one that knows, no-one, among the living.
Sea, sky, earth, everything here
Is doomed to disappear –
How could human soul escape from dying?
These are my thoughts:
New dawn will make all things right
When no longer the wolf the lam eats,

When no longer the brother his brother beats
And men do not grind their swords to fight

And all these lovely thoughts we dream
Must be turned into actions, actions that matter.
The calling of man is ideals to gather!
Or is this just a utopia?

The Song about Love

A sinful thought my brain huddles,

Twists like a snake circles.

One hand maiden's nipple fiddles

The other the loin cuddles.

White clothing black skin covers,

What a rich color mixture!

Black bosom, white snake in the picture.

Two true lovers!

What is More Beautiful?

What is more beautiful:
To believe that the freedom will begin,
To wish that enlightenment will win,
And to fight for enlightenment; -
Or to fight,
Knowing that dawn will not begin,
Knowing that freedom will not win,
And to keep on fighting?

What is more beautiful:
To think, if the freedom will not win,
To ponder, if dawn will not begin,
Why should one bother to fight at all?
Or to believe:
I'm the child of the sunset, not of the dawn,
Of enlightenment, though not as a winner born,
So, breaking up is my fate.

WINTER NIGHT (1905)

Nocturne

In my ears ring the corncrake's songs,
Above corn-ears full moon shines.
Summer-night's fortune to me belongs,
Smoke from burned clearing the meadow shields.
I'm not merry, I'm not sad, I don't weep,
But bring me the forest's shadows,
The shine of the cloud where the day drowns,
The shimmer of the windy hill still asleep,
Twinflower' fragrance, reflections on the lake;
The song of my heart from them I make.

I sing to you, virgin summer grass,
My heart's greatest solitude and silence,
My religion that celebrates a mass.
I will crown your head with laurels
I no longer search the will-o'-the wisp,

My hand holds the gold of happiness;

Around me the circle of life shrinks;

Time stands still, the weather-vane sleeps;

The road ahead is dim, I hardly see,

Dwelling unknown there waits for me.

Photo by Satu Runa

Windy Dwelling

Maiden, glowing red carnation,
Herb-garden's master creation,
Raised in a chamber tenderly,
Kept warm, cared for lovingly,
Yet you had a windy dwelling
On windowsill growing.

Maiden, glowing red carnation,
Summer's dream facing starvation
In the land of snow, blossoms a moment,
Withering abandoned
On the windowsill of the poet,
The window dark and vehement.

Rarely the sun there shined,
Even then through cracks in the walls;
Warmth there rarely stayed,
But misery constantly called;
Smiles into the dwelling rarely strayed,

Even then in the company of agony arrived.

Slandering Mouths

Bad mouths are slandering my lily,
Telling that she is silly
Calling my swan horse-haired loony.

They tell that you are proud.

Be proud, I'm proud also!
When you see the necks bowed
Your neck straight always hold.

You splash your life like a pond.

Keep splashing, so do I!
If the pond is shallow, muddy
Go around, stay lovely.

You waste smiles on your lips.

Waste your smiles, my girl, I also do!

The rich feel happy and wise

Looking down at others in despise.

When We Depart

Whenever I remember you,
The nightingales are singing
In the twilight of my evening.

Whenever you remember me,
The shrikes have their summer-fest,
They sit on my head to rest.

So, each other we remember;
Two lovely ones in the summer,
Summer leaf as the third.

The Fault

We both were in love, I loved you
And you loved me, that is true;
That was not the fault.

Both of us, each other we teased,
I teased you and you teased me;
That was not the fault.

There was a reason for this mishap:
Away from me you drifted,
My faults you recalled.

And another destruction seed:
Away from you I drifted;
I cried, my love.

*The Vine**

A hot climber was hugging me tight,
Wrapped me firm, the flower fiery, white,
In the fall-night's gloomy fragrance.

Breathing the thirst of the madness
The brain got drunk, head muddy, wet,
Temper tipsy, filled with badness,
An open fire on top of the head,
On the crown a bonfire burned,
The eyes in fire flamed,
The pupils shrank.

Blood vessels whizzed loud and raved,
And the midriff was nearly bursting,
The heart like a hot fire grate,
Like a spark-net the blood was boiling.

Chilling clear cold morning arrived;
My journey I wanted to start,

But my reason fell to the ground,

My heart fell, was never found

From the meadows of Lord's purple ward,

Among the purple march tea of the Lord.

---

*From Fire No.s 29/30, p 315, March 2008

Summer Morning

Seita Stockingmind
Was standing on a high clearing,
At dawn one summer morning.

Half asleep, half awake, charming
After sleeping a few dawn hours,
There slowly her slack joints stretching,
Crown adorned with summer-flowers.

The grass was tall, it hugged her knees,
Thick underbrush her thighs tickled,
Tips of hop-vine the waist embraced,
Sleepy poppy the bosom caressed,
She herself glowing like a rose
Above all others proudly awoke.

The beautiful fairy admired
The land and the ocean around her.

The honeybee, the man light in flight,
Flew to flower's bosom, inside;
Said Seita Stockingmind:
"Bad boy, stay away from my gown,
Don't open my petals, be so kind
My nectar is for midsummer night,
For someone who for me is right!"

The devilish bee warbled:
"My dear, let me your nectar gather,
I'm myself made of nectar's best matter
Of sugar turned into honey,
Your midsummer nectar I reap
But the honey for your feast you keep."

Seita Stockingmind,
Looked around with a quiet yawn,
Dew drops on her curls entwined,
In the red-glow of early dawn.

They Leave, Should I Grieve?

Fading like a mirage my dreams fly,
The dreams of my spirit have vanished,
Blown away to the backyards of sky,
To the hills of reality banished.

Should I regret, cry that they leave,
If banished, should I grieve?
Long enough have I watched the painting,
The rainbows of life adoring,
Walking deserts where the sand is dry,
Keeping my eyes on the blue of the sky.

Come-on, north wind, come and blow,
My oasis is green and calm.
Winter, cover my path with snow,
I see the sunny top of a palm.
Sing your mass, howl, storm of the Lord,
I hear cuckoo's harpsichord!

THE FROST (1908)

Sinikka's Song

Two boats in the bay of love float,

A ferry and a tiny boat.

    A cloud floats across the moon.

Tuoni's* ferry, ferry gruesome,

Rides the breakers, breakers awesome.

    A cloud floats across the moon.

The boat of dreams, its keel is frail,

It falters, shatters, bound to fail.

    A cloud floats across the moon.

Is it sadness, is it glee

Tuoni's ferry when I see?

    A cloud floats across the moon.

----

* Tuoni or Tuonela in Finnish mythology is the realm of death or underground.

Consolation of the Singer

My road has no ending
Though never reaching heaven.
Words and songs keep flying
Even in the gorge of raven.

Leaving home, sunshine, moon
I go to gorge's bottom.
Deepest darkness coming soon,
Smiling woman's bosom.

There you find no goodness,
Only hate and badness
And the loving deepest,
Fire of the night, the gloom darkest.

Decision

I will drop my load on the floor
Before the death comes to my door.

Leave the burden of scholarship,
Heavy millstone of craftsmanship.

To be under the heaven's dome,
In happiness of human home.

In paradise I thought was lost,
Away from death, away from frost.

Who am I, when that I know,
Then to the land of death I'll go.

Elegy*

Days of youth vanish
Like a stream rolling.
Grey is the fabric
In life's golden reed's weaving.
Futile, so futile to capture
A short moment's elation.
Company jolly, wine, celebration,
Bring no consolation.

Left behind, vanished
The proud, mighty days of my will.
Ecstatic spirit,
Joys of life banished.
From the ravine I climbed,
Is my road sinking again?
My only wish:
A brief moment's relief from pain.

I know that solace

In grave for me is waiting.
On the road of the searcher
No moment is granted for resting.
North-wind is blowing,
The sunset-clouds are stormy,
Leaving behind a red streak enchanted:
Feeble longing for beauty.

Sank into ocean
My blossoming roses and dreams.
The ransom for singing,
The poet is left with no means.
I did my utmost,
Could swing only a moment.
The gold of my dreams
Was paid with sorrows and torment.

I am exhausted,
Ah, to the roots of my heart!
Was the load carried
Too heavy from the very start?

Or am I a weakling

Though my will always was strong?

Victory empty,

Blamed by the deeds that were wrong.

In vain, ah in vain,

The crushing pains endured,

Heavy chains broken,

Boats beloved destroyed and burned.

Am I now falling,

When my wounds did finally heal?

When I need all I have,

Will I as an icicle freeze?

Against forces of heavens,

Hopeless, in vain, is the fight.

Echoes of kannel ring,

No longer sooth their child.

Freezing winds sing,

Tunes with broken wings swirl.

To the peace of my ravine

Like a beast dying I crawl.

----

*From Poetry Salzburg Review, p 67, No. 12, Autumn 2007

Visitor to Lapland

Forty below, biting frost, it's time to go.
High tax of Lapland – bloodstains in snow.

Your road leads high and my road goes low;
My soul follows where-ever you go.

Good bye to the rest by your bosom white,
To your eyes, fiery fox, in Lapland's night.

I wish to die without freedom's gift.
The sky is my father, my mother the snowdrift.

STARRY DOME (1912)

Two Kinds of Eyes

I once saw eyes that were sinful, tempting,
Eyes that were big, dark, and fire-striking,
Eyes that demanded all or nothing.
Next to them another pair of eyes was shining,
They were blue like the bluebell in the spring,
Demanding nothing, nothing,
Promising everything.

And I went with those sinful eyes, they won.
I gave them all I had, everything,
My home, my tribe, my happy work, all gone,
My pride, my peace, conscience, kept nothing,
Though I got nothing in return, nothing,
Giving to those eyes felt like a blessing.

Now again, two kinds of eyes to me shine

The eyes that are big, dark, full of sorrow,
Eyes enlarged by prolonged enduring pain,
And they motion, telling me: "tomorrow
Let's escape far away from here
A dignified new life we find there,
We start a new epoch, a new beginning,
Rising, and to rise each others helping,
To the highest heights of the Milky Way,
To the glory of sacred holy day!"

So to me they twinkled, those big dark eyes.
The other eyes too, were captivating,
Blue like a crack in newly frozen ice
Where the glitter of the sun is dancing:
"Come here, come here, let's dive in, arm in arm
We are young, rich pleasures are for us waiting,
Or if you won't, I will do no harm,
I shall kiss you as my royal highness,
I will give to you all my love, my charm –
Or kill, so the other eyes won't you caress!"

Times change, I too have changed though not bitter;

The eyes that now are big and sorrowful

Are the same as those that then were sinful –

The eyes that now so joyously glitter

And are sinful, belong to her best friend. –

Sinful eyes will again win, at the end.

The Insulted

Two slaves, together chained,
Deep to the heart insulted,
The wrists by shackles strained,
Shoulders heavily loaded!

We can't join together,
Separate neither,
We can't love each other,
We can't stop loving either.

My wrongful deeds were offending,
My heart was broken and crushed.
You wronged me, it was upsetting,
And my feelings were numbed.

So died also your sensuous feelings,
It was my fault that I know.
Gone are our happy spring-evenings,
Now eternal winter and snow.

When I see you again these days
Tears start flowing from my eyes,
Again, hand forsaken waves,
The heart forsaken, again dies.

I see that you too try to come near,
Trying to reach out towards me,
Then your heart's crying I hear
Though it once dared to hope and plea.

And then you pretend all is fine,
Again, hand offered stops waving,
All we have is memories' shrine,
Sorrow and mutual longing.

Two slaves, together chained,
Deep to the heart insulted,
In the wrists the shackles of love
Shoulders by wrongful deeds loaded!

Clearest Spring

Sweet spring, the clearest,
Tell me what to say
If my dearest
Meets me on the way?

Nothing, you just sigh,
Melt away and go,
Waste away and die
With the melting snow!

Spring, you are so clear
Tell me what to say,
If she will me spear,
Give me life today?

Nothing else is right
Enchanted you swear
An oath holy, white
Like the flowers in her hair!

Summer-Evening's Gentle Breeze

Summer-evening's breeze blows gently,
The tops of hillocks caress,
Woodlands path is silvery
In moonshine's charming finesse.

The woodland pines sway slowly,
Faraway cuckoo is calling,
The wanderer walks quietly,
The sorrows of his mind sleeping.

THE SUNSET (1914)

The Sunset

Ah sunset, why are you in such a hurry?
I'm tired, too tired to follow your flurry,
So much work still remains, much effort and fight,
I'm scared of the endless night.

»You unhappy child, play if the pace you can't keep!
Nobody catches my stallions' leap.
But if to reach your dream is your fancy and will
You must run fast, much faster still.

Ah sunset, to leap with your stallions is my yearning,
But my strength is already straining,
The stones on the road, the stumps make me stumble,
My body is weak and starts to fumble.

»You senseless man, give up now, abandon your goal,

Your spirit's longing will destroy your soul!
A journey this long you should always start early,
Abandon now your hopeless journey.

Ah sunset, I started in the early morning,
As a child I was flaming and burning,
Not yet do I want into ashes to burn,
Some daylight from you I wish to earn.

»You poor human, to that generation you belong
That wasn't blessed with sleep, awake all night long,
So struggle and strike in the sunset's glow,
I will leave behind a glittering bow.

O sunset, I ask you, I beg you, I demand,
Wait until my last song is ready, I command!
I am almost finished, not often I pray,
Just one moment in daylight to stay.

The sunset arrived and arrived the night,
An arch in the horizon glitters so bright.

Out in the backwoods, dark night tells a story,

The song about work and its glory.

Photo by Asa Lyytinen

Autumn Leaves

Autumn leaves are flying overhead,
Sorrow is booming in wanderer's chest.

- Flying leaf, my fate like yours will it be,
The end of my love and my singing I see?

»Stranger, don't worry, our newfound brother!
Thousands of years or a moment doesn't matter.

- Flying leaf, like you, am I left floating free,
Detached from my life, from my pleasure-tree?

»Just stay calm! Life is a dream, not to keep.
Your only joy: cry for your dream when you sleep.

- Flying leaf, like you can I fly, like a swan,
  Fading to dreams of the rising dawn?

»Smarten up, our newfound brother!

New dawn will come, not your sorrow.

The leaves fly over poor wanderer's head
Who still longs for the beauty he once met.

THE BEAUTY OF LIFE (1915)

The Swells

Like shallow gentle waves
The storms of my mind swell,
Dreams and escapades,
As memories still dwell.

Many years I aged in just a few months.
How did I learn that to know?
Because I noticed that I had learned
To take insults without a row.

Because now the sorrows of the spirit
Are stronger than my feelings' fires.
Now pleasures I deny from myself
Though newer denied your desires.

Lovely, sunny days ahead?

Perhaps, perhaps a canyon deep,

Death, poverty, misery, perhaps –

Or death on a manure-heap.

What is important to others

Means nothing to me, just a boredom,

The riches, love, honor and power,

Only my spirit's eternal freedom.

CAMPFIRES (1917)

Evening Sentiment

The sunset in faraway backwoods
On the lakes golden shimmer creates.
Still brighter is shimmer of bulrush,
And the island's point and the straits.

Ah, my chest restless, if only
From here it would find the peace,
As if hopes had never existed,
Forgetting the memories!

That gold of the sun, if only
Inside one's heart one could take,
And to himself to be a stranger
Like the bulrush and glittering lake!

LOVE SONGS (1919)

I Wander the Trails in the Forest

*On paths in the forest I wander
Deep in my thoughts one summer evening,
My chest swells with joy, and I ponder,
Singing, singing and humming.*

*There, in the grove's verdant splendor
Something strange happened to me,
So gentle and so tender,
In the fragrance of bird-cherry tree.*

*I'm the one and the only to know,
Someone else it knows, and just me,
And the ladybird in the grove
And the fragrant bird-cherry tree.*

Those Eyes

Those eyes of happiness sparkled
So furious, so charming.
Those eyes of merriment crackled,
So strangely undulating.

Was that strange sparkle your happiness
Since by birth you were a flower?
You threw fire into my feelings,
Facing you my will lost its power.

Or was that glow from the happiness
That my whole life I searched?
Asking, inviting to come close,
And it always like an echo faded.

WHEN THE LILACS ARE BLOSSOMING, 1920

Autumn Morning

Frosty silvery veils, long, opalescent
Over the fields are clinging,
Over the yellowish land and forest,
On tree branches swinging.

The sun is already rising,
Time for me to follow.
I sit quietly longing
By my cabin's window.

I see the road and the red milestone,
Sunrise's majestic show.
I see the field and the forest,
The thicket of crack willow.

I see my whole life, the future and the past –

Ah, it makes me shiver!
Cruel torment of happiness lost,
My heart starts to tremble.

Ah, opalescent frosty silvery veils
Cover my paining core
So that the forsaken love's shadow
Will not sneak to my door;
So that the calls of the lonely soul
Not just the shadow hears,
And the pillowcase of this poor man
Would not be covered by tears.

SHEMEIKA'S SORROW (1924)

The Goodness

The Goodness arrives, she makes no noise,
She walks and whispers with silent voice.

Her voice is the voice of suffering,
She has cried for us, agonizing.

In her eyes she has desperate views,
Still they are filled with hope-giving news.

For you, she offers the pearls she wears,
It's all that she has and that's all she cares.

Take her gift as a divine pleasure,
From heaven's valleys comes this treasure.

She came to you to sooth your cries,

And she wants to look deep in your eyes,

And caress your hand and go away,
Whispering: there will be a better day.

Photo by Satu Runa

The Child of July

The life without love is not worth living,
My mother was so gentle and loving.
I'm longing for love and affection
To warm up in flames of compassion.

Blown to foreign shores by hostile gales,
Where freezing winds haul.
Gloomy hymns sing their tales,
And sorrows the heart maul.

On the brightest July day I was born,
I long for the days that were worm and nice.
Those mocking mouths, I can't take their scorn
Those icy glances, filled with despise.
I love the song of the trees in the valleys,
Not the highland wind that blows in these alleys.

The Sickle of the Moon

Like the sickle of the moon
Shifts in the night forlorn,
Your love cuts my heart like harpoon,
Its lentil and its corn.
Just like a wisp of a cloud
To the northern sky confined,
I have a dream in a shroud,
In my sorrowful mind.

No right I have of love to dream,
For sure not, that I know.
The jamb of my night got dim
Like the evening-cloud's glow.
I grew old and became strange,
My mind turned dark like the night,
My thoughts and my outlook of life
Filled with horror and fright.

Delusion

Like the rising sun she arrived,
Like destiny, moonshine in the night.
Her eyes looked at me enquiring
With a cold and holy questioning.

Those eyes looked deep into my soul
Like into a gorge, a throat, a hole,
Perhaps bad, evil things they observed,
Because after that, they never returned.

Or was she heaven's delusion,
Drowning my road like an illusion?
She was leading me, I went astray,
Is she with me, or did she go away?

A REMEMBERANCE, 1925

*1. **The Star***

Did you fall, straying too far?
My life's golden star.

She is gone, out of sight,
The loveliest one in the night.

She didn't die; she was captured by vanity,
Left alone, night covers the lonely.

Is my fate like yours – nothing can me save.
Hauling wolf pack is circling my grave.

I ask only this, I beg only this:
A peaceful rest, my only wish!

You are gone, never returning
Remembering you, my sorrows are crying.

2. *The Ray and the Crystal*

My ice-cold mind perhaps exploded
On that flaming pond's icy surface,
In ecstasy insane it bombarded
Icy waves, in frozen embrace.

The nature's laws tell: if the spring days,
The fall and the crystal ray
Seek their happiness under the waves,
Their destiny: frozen decay.

That's why the rage of my suffering,
Like a captive of wind and fire.
The golden bubble glittering
Like the snow of death and winter.

3. *Swan lake*

Perhaps I was on Golden sunrays riding,
Perhaps the waves of the summer-night gliding.

Can't recall if it was evening or dawn,
White hue reminded me of the swan.

Shadowless light filled my mind with brightness,
Like the chest of the swan, the whiteness.

My midsummer dreams the swans were singing,
Of my first love, its sensuous dreaming.

But when I tried to approach them, away they flew
Like the wisp of a cloud with a whitish hue.